The Quotable Writer: Writers on the Writers Life

By

Richard W. Willoughby

A

I love deadlines. I like the whooshing sound they make as they fly by.
Douglas Adams

There are two kinds of writer: those that make you think, and those that make you wonder. **Brian Aldiss**

A writer should say to himself, not, How can I get more money?, but How can I reach more readers (without lowering standards)? **Brian Aldiss**

The story...must be a conflict, and specifically, a conflict between the forces of good and evil within a single person. **Maxwell Anderson**

When a man publishes a book, there are so many stupid things said that he declares he'll never do it again. The praise is almost always worse than the criticism. **Sherwood Anderson**

You know how it is in the kid's book world; it's just bunny eat bunny.
Anonymous

Character gives us qualities, but it is in actions - what we do - that we are happy or the reverse....All human happiness and misery take the form of action.
Aristotle

Have something to say, and say it as clearly as you can. That is the only secret.
Matthew Arnold

It is the writer who might catch the imagination of young people, and plant a seed that will flower and come to fruition. **Isaac Asimov**

No one suggests that writing about science will turn the entire world into a model of judgment and creative thought. It will be enough if they spread the knowledge as widely as possible. **Isaac Asimov**

Rejection slips, or form letters, however tactfully phrased, are lacerations of the soul, if not quite inventions of the devil - but there is no way around them. **Isaac Asimov**

To most readers the word 'fiction' is an utter fraud. They are entirely convinced that each character has an exact counterpart in real life and that any small discrepancy with that counterpart is a simple error on the author's part. Consequently, they are totally at a loss if anything essential is altered. Make Abraham Lincoln a dentist, put the Gettysburg Address on his tongue, and nobody will recognize it. **Louis Auchincloss**

B

The only thing I was fit for was to be a writer, and this notion rested solely on my suspicion that I would never be fit for real work, and that writing didn't require any. **Russell Baker**

Unless a writer is extremely old when he dies, in which case he has probably become a neglected institution, his death must always be seen as untimely. This is because a real writer is always shifting and changing and searching. The world has many labels for him, of which the most treacherous is the label of Success. **James Baldwin**

If the artist does not fling himself, without reflecting, into his work, as Curtis flung himself into the yawning gulf, as the soldier flings himself into the enemy's trenches, and if, once in this crater, he does not work like a miner on whom the walls of his gallery have fallen in; if he contemplates difficulties instead of overcoming them one by one...he is simply looking on at the suicide of his own talent. **Honore de Balzac**

It took me fifteen years to discover I had no talent for writing, but I couldn't give it up because by that time I was too famous. **Robert Benchley**

Why do writers write? Because it isn't there. **Thomas Berger**

He was such a bad writer, they revoked his poetic license. **Milton Berle**

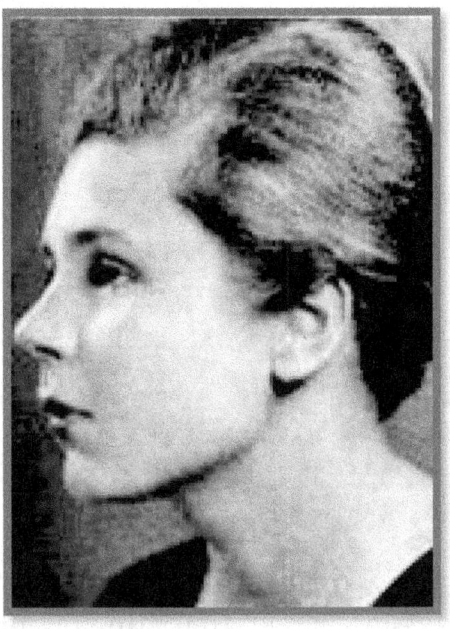

And as to experience--well, think how little some good poets have had, or how much some bad ones have. **Elizabeth Bishop**

Being a poet is one of the unhealthier jobs--no regular hours, so many temptations! **Elizabeth Bishop**

A best seller was a book which somehow sold well simply because it was selling well. **S. Boorstein**

In science there is a dictum: don't add an experiment to an experiment. Don't make things unnecessarily complicated. In writing fiction, the more fantastic the tale, the plainer the prose should be. Don't ask your readers to admire your words when you want them to believe your story. **Ben Bova**

There is probably no hell for authors in the next world -- they suffer so much from critics and publishers in this. **C. N. Bovee**

Bring all your intelligence to bear on your beginning. **Elizabeth Bowen**

Any man who keeps working is not a failure. He may not be a great writer, but if he applies the old-fashioned virtues of hard, constant labor, he'll eventually make some kind of career for himself as writer. **Ray Bradbury**

First, find out what your hero wants, then just follow him! **Ray Bradbury**

Beware of self-indulgence. The romance surrounding the writing profession carries several myths: that one must suffer in order to be creative; that one must be cantankerous and objectionable in order to be bright; that ego is paramount over skill; that one an rise to a level from which one can tell the reader to go to hell. These myths, if believed, can ruin you. If you believe you can make a living as a writer, you already have enough ego. **David Brin**

If you have other things in your life -- family, friends, good productive day work -- these can interact with your writing and the sum will be all the richer. **David Brin**

The writer is important only by dint of the territory he colonizes. **Van Wyck Brooks**

Either a writer doesn't want to talk about his work, or he talks about it more than you want. **Anatole Broyard**

Sex almost always disappoints me in novels. Everything can be said or done now, and that's what I often find: everything, a feeling of generality or dispersal. But in my experience, true sex is so particular, so peculiar to the person who yearns for it. Only he or she, and no one else, would desire so very much that very person under those circumstances. In fiction, I miss that sense of terrific specificity.
Anatole Broyard

Don't explain why it works; explain how you use it. **Steven Brust**

Literature is all, or mostly, about sex. **Anthony Burgess**

Style has always been in my mind the author's Self, the creative expression of that Self. **Whit Burnett**

I have been successful probably because I have always realized that I knew nothing about writing and have merely tried to tell an interesting story entertainingly. **Edgar Rice Burroughs**

If you write one story, it may be bad; if you write a hundred, you have the odds in your favor. **Edgar Rice Burroughs**

C

The reason 99% of all stories written are not bought by editors is very simple. Editors never buy manuscripts that are left on the closet shelf at home. **John Campbell**

Finishing a book is just like you took a child out in the back yard and shot it. **Truman Capote**

I believe more in the scissors than I do in the pencil. **Truman Capote**

Everybody walks past a thousand story ideas every day. The good writers are the ones who see five or six of them. Most people don't see any. **Orson Scott Card**

Short stories are designed to deliver their impact in as few pages as possible. A tremendous amount is left out, and a good short story writer learns to include only the most essential information. **Orson Scott Card**

Most of the basic material a writer works with is acquired before the age of fifteen. **Willa Cather**

Coleridge was a drug addict. Poe was an alcoholic. Marlowe was killed by a man whom he was treacherously trying to stab. Pope took money to keep a woman's name out of a satire then wrote a piece so that she could still be recognized anyhow. Chatterton killed himself. Byron was accused of incest. Do you still want to a writer--and if so, why? **Bennett Cerf**

If you look at anything long enough, say just that wall in front of you -- it will come out of that wall. **Anton Chekhov**

My own experience is that once a story has been written, one has to cross out the beginning and the end. It is there that we authors do most of our lying. **Anton Chekhov**

When men ask me how I know so much about men, they get a simple answer: everything I know about men, I learned from me. **Anton Chekhov**

It is perfectly okay to write garbage--as long as you edit brilliantly. **C. J. Cherryh**

Next to doing things that deserve to be written, nothing gets a man more credit, or gives him more pleasure than to write things that deserve to be read. **Lord Chesterfield**

I've always believed in writing without a collaborator, because when two people are writing the same book, each believes he gets all the worries and only half the royalties. **Agatha Christie**

I firmly believe every book was meant to be written. **Marchette Chute**

The spirit of creation is the spirit of contradiction. It is the breakthrough of appearances toward an unknown reality. **Jean Cocteau**

Every great and original writer, in proportion as he is great or original, must himself create the taste by which he is to be relished. **Samuel Taylor Coleridge**

Put down everything that comes into your head and then you're a writer. But an author is one who can judge his own stuff's worth, without pity, and destroy most of it. **Colette**

My task...is, by the power of the written word to make you hear, to make you feel - it is, before all, to make you see. That - and no more - and it is everything. Joseph Conrad

Only in men's imagination does every truth find an effective and undeniable existence. Imagination, not invention, is the supreme master of art as of life. Joseph Conrad

A writer without interest or sympathy for the foibles of his fellow man is not conceivable as a writer. Joseph Conrad

There are three difficulties in authorship: to write anything worth publishing -- to find honest men to publish it -- and to get sensible men to read it. Charles Caleb Colton

Books aren't written, they're rewritten. Including your own. It is one of the hardest things to accept, especially after the seventh rewrite hasn't quite done it... **Michael Crichton**

Most writers can write books faster than publishers can write checks. **Richard Curtis**

D

Never throw up on an editor. **Ellen Datlow**

In writing a series of stories about the same characters, plan the whole series in advance in some detail, to avoid contradictions and inconsistencies. **L. Sprague de Camp**

There is no mistaking the dismay on the face of a writer who has just heard that his brain child is a deformed idiot. **L. Sprague de Camp**

The imagination is the spur of delights...all depends upon it, it is the mainspring of everything; now, is it not by the means of the imagination one knows joy? Is it not of the imagination that the sharpest pleasures arise? **Marquis DeSade**

Every novel should have a beginning, a middle, and an end. **Peter De Vries**

I love being a writer. What I can't stand is the paperwork. **Peter de Vries**

Make everybody fall out of the plane first, and then explain who they were and why they were in the plane to begin with. **Nancy Ann Dibble**

Science fiction writers, I am sorry to say, really do not know anything. We can't talk about science, because our knowledge of it is limited and unofficial, and usually our fiction is dreadful. **Philip K. Dick**

A word is dead
When it is said,
Some say.
I say it just begins
to live that day.
Emily Dickinson

Writers are always selling somebody out. **Joan Didion**

What we call fiction is the ancient way of knowing, the total discourse that antedates all the special vocabularies....Fiction is democratic, it reasserts the authority of the single mind to make and remake the world. **E. L. Doctorow**

Writing a novel is like driving a car at night. You can only see as far as your headlights, but you can make the whole trip that way. **E. L. Doctorow**

Writing is turning one's worst moments into money. **J. P. Donleavy**

As for me, this is my story: I worked and was tortured. You know what it means to compose? No, thank God, you do not! I believe you have never written to order, by the yard, and have never experienced that hellish torture. **Fyodor Dostoevsky**

An excellent precept for writers: have a clear idea of all the phrases and expressions you need, and you will find them. **Ximenes Doudan**

If it has horses and swords in it, it's a fantasy, unless it also has a rocketship in it, in which case it becomes science fiction. The only thing that'll turn a story with a rocketship in it back into fantasy is the Holy Grail. **Debra Doyle**

To write good SF today...you must push further and harder, reach deeper into your own mind until you break through into the strange and terrible country wherein live your own dreams. **Gardner Dozois**

E

If you start with a bang, you won't end with a whimper. **T.S. Eliot**

There is no method except to be very intelligent. **T. S. Eliot**

People do not deserve to have good writing, they are so pleased with bad. **Ralph Waldo Emerson**

The virtue of books is to be readable. **Ralph Waldo Emerson**

Nothing, not love, not greed, not passion or hatred, is stronger than a writer's need to change another writer's copy. **Arthur Evans**

F

At one time I thought the most important thing was talent. I think now that the young man or the young woman must possess or teach himself, training himself, in infinite patience, which is to try and to try until it comes right. He must train himself in ruthless intolerance--that is to throw away anything that is false no matter how much he might love that page or that paragraph. The most important thing is insight, that is to be--curiosity--to wonder, to mull, and to muse why it is that man does what he does, and if you have that, then I don't think the talent makes much difference, whether you've got it or not. **William Faulkner**

Get it down. Take chances. It may be bad, but it's the only way you can do anything really good. **William Faulkner**

It begins with a character, usually, and once he stands up on his feet and begins to move, all I can do is trot along behind him with a paper and pencil trying to keep up long enough to put down what he says and does. **William Faulkner**

The work never matches the dream of perfection the artist has to start with. **William Faulkner**

There is no idea so brilliant or original that a sufficiently-untalented writer can't screw it up. **Raymond Feist**

The ideal view for daily writing, hour for hour, is the blank brick wall of a cold-storage warehouse. Failing this, a stretch of sky will do, cloudless if possible.
Edna Ferber

To the composition of novels and romances, nothing is necessary but paper, pens, and ink, with the manual capacity of using them. Henry Fielding

Begin with an individual, and before you know it you have created a type; begin with a type, and you find you have created - nothing. F. Scott Fitzgerald

Draw your chair up close to the edge of the precipice and I'll tell you a story. -F. Scott Fitzgerald

Find the key emotion; this may be all you need know to find your short story. F. Scott Fitzgerald

To have something to say is a question of sleepless nights and worry and endless ratiocination of a subject - of endless trying to dig out of the essential truth, the essential justice. F. Scott Fitzgerald

I am irritated by my own writing. I am like a violinist whose ear is true, but whose fingers refuse to reproduce precisely the sound he hears within. Gustave Flaubert

Observe, don't imitate. John M. Ford

The historian records, but the novelist creates. E. M. Forster

A novel must give a sense of permanence as well as a sense of life. E. M. Forster

Suspense: the only literary tool that has any effect upon tyrants and savages. E. M. Forster

Don't be dismayed by the opinions of editors, or critics. They are only the traffic cops of the arts. Gene Fowler

Writing is easy; all you do is sit staring at a blank sheet of paper until the drops of blood form on your forehead. **Gene Fowler**

To know is nothing at all; to imagine is everything. **Anatole France**

If you would not be forgotten,
as soon as you are dead and rotten,
either write things worth reading,
or do things worth the writing.
Benjamin Franklin

The greatest rules of dramatic writing are conflict, conflict, conflict. **James Frey**

Style is less the man than the way a man takes himself. **Robert Frost**

An artist's sensitivity to criticism is, at least in part, an effort to keep unimpaired the zest, or confidence, or arrogance, which he needs to make creation possible; or an instinct to climb through his problems in his own way as he should, and must. **Christopher Fry**

G

When writing a novel, that's pretty much entirely what life turns into: 'House burned down. Car stolen. Cat exploded. Did 1500 easy words, so all in all it was a pretty good day.' Neil Gaiman

In nearly all good fiction, the basic - all but inescapable - plot form is this: A central character wants something, goes after it despite opposition (perhaps including his own doubts), and so arrives at a win, lose, or draw. John Gardner

If you haven't got an idea, start a story anyway. You can always throw it away, and maybe by the time you get to the fourth page you will have an idea, and you'll only have to throw away the first three pages. **William Campbell Gault**

Half of being smart is knowing what you're dumb at. **David Gerrold**

There is more pleasure to building castles in the air than on the ground.
Edward Gibbon

Often with good sentiments we produce bad literature. Andre Gide

Whatever you can do, or dream you can, begin it; Boldness has genius, power and magic in it. Johann Wolfgang von Goethe

In brief, I spend half my time trying to learn the secrets of other writers -- to apply them to the expression of my own thoughts. **Shirley Ann Grau**

There's no money in poetry, but then there's no poetry in money either. **Robert Graves**

Instead of marveling with Johnson, how anything but profit should incite men to literary labor, I am rather surprised that mere emolument should induce them to labor so well. **Thomas Green**

Plotting is like sex. Plotting is about desire and satisfaction, anticipation and release. You have to arouse your reader's desire to know what happens, to unravel the mystery, to see good triumph. You have to sustain it, keep it warm, feed it, just a little bit, not too much at a time, as your story goes on. That's called suspense. It can bring desire to a frenzy, in which case you are in a good position to bring off a wonderful climax. Colin Greenland

Plotting isn't like sex, because you can go back and adjust it afterwards. Whether you plan your story beforehand or not, if the climax turns out to be the revelation that the mad professor's anti-gravity device actually works, you must go back and silently delete all those flying cars buzzing around the city on page one. If you want to reveal something, you need to hide it properly first. Colin Greenland

A writer will seal his own coffin,
And the interests of readers will soften,
If the author insists
On the usual twists,
And he goes to the Wells once too often.
Mark Grenier

The writer's genetic inheritance and her or his experiences shape the writer into a unique individual, and it is this uniqueness that is the writer's only stuff for sale. **James Gunn**

H

Asking a working writer what he thinks about critics is like asking a lamppost how it feels about dogs. **Christopher Hampton**

Put weather in. Joseph Hansen

It's better to write about things you feel than about things you know about.
L. P. Hartley

Don't use metaphors in fantasy; your readers will take them literally. Or they may take them figuratively -- but if so, they'll also take your magics and transformations figuratively. Either way, you're in trouble. Teresa Nielsen Hayden

The essence of drama is that man cannot walk away from the consequences of his own deeds. Harold Hayes

Writing is not necessarily something to be ashamed of, but do it in private and wash your hands afterwards. **Robert A. Heinlein**

In a good play, everyone is in the right. **Fredrich Hebbel**

All good books are alike in that they are truer than if they had really happened and after you are finished reading one you will feel that all that happened to you and afterwards it all belongs to you; the good and the bad, the ecstasy, the remorse and sorrow, the people and the places and how the weather was. If you can get so that you can give that to people, then you are a writer. **Ernest Hemingway**

Easy writing makes hard reading. **Ernest Hemingway**

If a writer of prose knows enough about what he is writing about he may omit things that he knows and the reader, if the writer is writing truly enough, will have a feeling of those things as strongly as though the writer had stated them. The dignity of movement of an iceberg is due to only one-eighth of it being above water. A writer who omits things because he does not know them only makes hollow places in his writing. **Ernest Hemingway**

It's none of their business that you have to learn to write. Let them think you were born that way. **Ernest Hemingway**

My aim is to put down what I see and what I feel in the best and simplest way I can tell it. **Ernest Hemingway**

Prose is architecture, not interior decoration. **Ernest Hemingway**

Manuscript: something submitted in haste and returned at leisure. **Oliver Herford**

To be a writer is to sit down at one's desk in the chill portion of every day, and to write; not waiting for the little jet of the blue flame of genius to start from the breastbone - just plain going at it, in pain and delight. To be a writer is to throw away a great deal, not to be satisfied, to type again, and then again, and once more, and over and over.... **John Hersey**

I never dare to write as funny as I can. **Oliver Wendell Holmes**

What a blessed thing it is that nature, when she invented, manufactured and patented her authors, contrived to make critics out of the chips that were left! **Oliver Wendell Holmes**

Editor: A person employed by a newspaper, whose business it is to separate the wheat from the chaff, and to see that the chaff is printed. **Elbert Hubbard**

Only a person with a Best Seller mind can write Best Sellers. **Aldous Huxley**

To write fiction, one needs a whole series of inspirations about people in an actual environment, and then a whole lot of work on the basis of those inspirations. **Aldous Huxley**

I

A writer never has a vacation. For a writer life consists of either writing or thinking about writing. **Eugene Ionesco**

Half my life is an act of revision. **John Irving**

The literary world is made up of little confederacies, each looking upon its own members as the lights of the universe; and considering all others as mere transient meteors, doomed to soon fall and be forgotten, while its own luminaries are to shine steadily into immortality. **Washington Irving**

J

Make him [the reader] think the evil, make him think it for himself, and you are released from weak specifications. **Henry James**

What is either a picture or a novel that is not character? **Henry James**

Writing is not primarily escape, but use. Henry James

As long as mixed grills and combination salads are popular, anthologies will undoubtedly continue in favor. Elizabeth Janeway

The most valuable of all talents is that of never using two words when one will do. Thomas Jefferson

Sir, nobody but a blockhead ever wrote except for money. **Samuel Johnson**

Abuse is often of service. There is nothing so dangerous to an author as silence. **Samuel Johnson**

It is advantageous to an author that his book should be attacked as well as praised. Fame is a shuttlecock. If it be struck at one end of the room, it will soon fall to the ground. To keep it up, it must be struck at both ends. **Samuel Johnson**

...it will not always happen that the success of a poet is proportionate to his labor. **Samuel Johnson**

Tediousness is the most fatal of all faults. **Samuel Johnson**

Genius is not a quality, but only a quantitative difference in a combination of attributes contained in all persons. **Dr. Ernst Jones**

Honest criticism is hard to take, particularly from a relative, a friend, an acquaintance, or a stranger. **Franklin Jones**

I went for years not finishing anything. Because, of course, when you finish something you can be judged...I had poems which were re-written so many times I suspect it was just a way of avoiding sending them out. **Erica Jong**

The artist is not a person endowed with free will who seeks his own ends, but one who allows art to realize its supreme purpose through him. **Carl Jung**

K

I get up in the morning, torture a typewriter until it screams, then stop.
Clarence Budington Kelland

Confronted by an absolutely infuriating review it is sometimes helpful for the victim to do a little personal research on the critic. Is there any truth to the rumor that he had no formal education beyond the age of eleven? In any event, is he able to construct a simple English sentence? Do his participles dangle? When moved to lyricism does he write "I had a fun time"? Was he ever arrested for burglary? I don't know that you will prove anything this way, but it is perfectly harmless and quite soothing. **Jean Kerr**

I am a part of all I have read. **John Kieran**

If you would write emotionally, be first unemotional. If you would move your readers to tears, do not let them see you cry. **James J. Kilpatrick**

I try to create sympathy for my characters, then turn the monsters loose.
Stephen King

Close the door. Write with no one looking over your shoulder. Don't try to figure out what other people want to hear from you; figure out what you have to say. It's the one and only thing you have to offer. **Barbara Kingsolver**

This manuscript of yours that has just come back from another editor is a precious package. Don't consider it rejected. Consider that you've addressed it 'to the editor who can appreciate my work' and it has simply come back stamped 'Not at this address'. Just keep looking for the right address. **Barbara Kingsolver**

Use your imagination. Trust me, your lives are not interesting. Don't write them down. W. B. Kinsella

I keep six honest serving men
(They taught me all I knew);
Their names are What and Why and When
and How and Where and Who.
Rudyard Kipling

There are nine and sixty ways
Of constructing tribal lays,
And every single one of them is right!
Rudyard Kipling

Words are the most powerful drug used by mankind. Rudyard Kipling

Poets are interested mostly in death and commas. Carolyn Kizer

The trouble with science fiction is that you can write about everything: time, space, all the future, all the past, all of the universe, any kind of creature imaginable. That's too big. It provides no focus for the artist. An artist needs, in order to function, some narrowing of focus. Usually, in the history of art, the narrower the focus in which the artist is forced to work, the greater the art. Philip Klass

Science fiction is what I point at when I say science fiction. Damon Knight

Fiction is about stuff that's screwed up. Nancy Kress

L

In general...there's no point in writing hopeless novels. We all know we're going to die; what's important is the kind of men and women we are in the face of this. Anne Lamott

We are a species that needs and wants to understand who we are. Sheep lice do not seem to share this longing, which is one reason why they write so little. Anne Lamott

Writing is a fairly lonely business unless you invite people in to watch you do it, which is often distracting and then have to ask them to leave. Marc Lawrence

Having been unpopular in high school is not just cause for book publication. Fran Lebowitz

If science fiction is the mythology of modern technology, then its myth is tragic. Ursula K. Le Guin

In the tale, in the telling, we are all one blood. Take the tale in your teeth, then, and bite till the blood runs, hoping it's not poison; and we will all come to the end together, and even to the beginning: living, as we do, in the middle. Ursula K. Le Guin

The unread story is not a story; it is little black marks on wood pulp. The reader, reading it, makes it live: a live thing, a story. Ursula K. Le Guin

That's the essential goal of the writer: you slice out a piece of yourself and slap it down on the desk in front of you. You try to put it on paper, try to describe it in a way that the reader can see and feel and touch. You paste all your nerve endings into it and then give it out to strangers who don't know you or understand you. And you will feel everything that happens to that story -- if they like it, if they hate it. Because no matter how you try to distance yourself from it, to some degree you feel that if they hate it, they hate you. Which isn't the truth, you understand. At least you understand that in your head...but not always in your heart. Stephen Leigh

You may be able to take a break from writing, but you won't be able to take a break from being a writer... Stephen Leigh

All the information you need can be given in dialogue. **Elmore Leonard**

The writer who cannot sometimes throw away a thought about which another man would have written dissertations, without worry whether or not the reader will find it, will never become a great writer. **Georg Christoph Lichtenberg**

Great is the art of beginning, but greater is the art of ending. **Henry Wadsworth Longfellow**

ny magazine-cover hack can splash paint around wildly and call it a nightmare, or a witches sabbath or a portrait of the devil; but only a great painter can make such a thing really scare or ring true. That's because only a real artist knows the anatomy of the terrible, or the physiology of fear. H. P. Lovecraft

Nature fits all her children with something to do, he who would write and can't write, can surely review. James Russell Lowell

M

James Blish told me I had the worst case of "said bookism" (that is, using every word except said to indicate dialogue). He told me to limit the verbs to said, replied, asked, and answered and only when absolutely necessary. **Anne McCaffrey**

Tell the readers a story! Because without a story, you are merely using words to prove you can string them together in logical sentences. **Anne McCaffrey**

Writing is not a genteel profession; it's quite nasty and tough and kind of dirty. **Rosemary Mahoney**

The task of a writer consists in being able to make something out of an idea.
Thomas Mann

A critic knows more than the author he criticizes, or just as much, or at least somewhat less. **Cardinal Manning**

If you go too far in fantasy and break the string of logic, and become nonsensical, someone will surely remind you of your dereliction....Pound for pound, fantasy makes a tougher opponent for the creative person. **Richard Matheson**

All the words I use in my stories can be found in the dictionary -- it's just a matter of arranging them into the right sentences. Somerset Maugham

If you can tell stories, create characters, devise incidents, and have sincerity and passion, it doesn't matter a damn how you write. Somerset Maugham

There are three rules for writing. Unfortunately, no one can agree what they are. Somerset Maugham

We do not write because we want to; we write because we have to. Somerset Maugham

To produce a mighty book, you must choose a mighty theme. Herman Melville

You write that first draft really to see how it's going to come out. James A. Michener

A person who publishes a book willfully appears before the populace with his pants down...If it is a good book nothing can hurt him. If it is a bad book, nothing can help him. Edna St. Vincent Millay

Writing is its own reward. Henry Miller

Almost anyone can be an author; the business is to collect money and fame from this state of being. A. A. Milne

When you take stuff from one writer, it's plagiarism; but when you take it from many writers, it's research. William Mizner

I wonder why murder is considered less immoral than fornication in literature. George Moore

No tears in the writer, no tears in the reader. George Moore

A man is a writer if all his words are strung in definite sentence sounds.
Marianne Moore

Anecdotes don't make good stories. Generally I dig down underneath them so far
that the story that finally comes out is not what people thought their anecdotes
were about. Alice Munro

I have a theory of my own about what the art of the novel is, and how it came into
being....It happens because the storyteller's own experience...has moved him to
an emotion so passionate that he can no longer keep it shut up in his heart.
Lady Murasaki

N

I have written - often several times - every word I have ever published.
Vladimir Nabokov

Only ambitious nonentities and hearty mediocrities exhibit their rough drafts. It's like passing around samples of sputum. **Vladimir Nabokov**

Don't sell yourself short; dare to dream. You might sell to a top market before you ever sell to a non-paying market - you won't know unless you try. In the same way, it's good to be cooperative, but don't be too humble either. **Rheal Nadeau**

I'm the kind of writer that people think other people are reading. **V. S. Naipaul**

The author must keep his mouth shut when his work starts to speak. **Frederich Nietzsche**

We write to taste life twice, in the moment and in retrospection. **Anais Nin**

The reader has certain rights. He bought your story. Think of this as an implicit contract. He's entitled to be entertained, instructed, amused; maybe all three. If he quits in the middle, or puts the book down feeling his time has been wasted, you're in violation. **Larry Niven**

You learn by writing short stories. Keep writing short stories. The money's in novels, but writing short stories keeps your writing lean and pointed. **Larry Niven**

O

If you do not have an alert and curious interest in character and dramatic situation, if you have no visual imagination and are unable to distinguish between honest emotional reactions and sentimental approaches to life, you will never write a competent short story. **Edward J. O'Brien**

Everywhere I go I'm asked if I think the university stifles writers. My opinion is that they don't stifle enough of them. **Flannery O'Connor**

The framework of the artist's ideas is clearly only that which he is forever seeking for universality, and must be far wider than the framework of the ideals of the patriot. **Sean O'Faolain**

All writers are vain, selfish and lazy, and at the very bottom of their motives lies a mystery. Writing a book is a long, exhausting struggle, like a long bout of some painful illness. One would never undertake such a thing if one were not driven by some demon whom one can neither resist nor understand. **George Orwell**

One hasn't become a writer until one has distilled writing into a habit, and that habit has been forced into an obsession. Writing has to be an obsession. It has to be something as organic, physiological and psychological as speaking or sleeping or eating. **Niyi Osundare**

All a poet can do is warn. **Wilfred Owen**

No tale tells all. **Alexei Panshin**

I can't write five words but that I change seven. **Dorothy Parker**

Everything that is written merely to please the author is worthless. **Blaise Pascal**

When we see a natural style we are quite amazed and delighted, because we expected to see an author and find a man. **Blaise Pascal**

The best way to have a good idea is to have lots of ideas. **Linus Pauling**

Make it new. **Ezra Pound**

Fantasy doesn't have to be fantastic. American writers in particular find this much harder to grasp. You need to have your feet on the ground as much as your head in the clouds. The cute dragon that sits on your shoulder also craps all down your back, but this makes it more interesting because it gives it an added dimension. **Terry Pratchett**

There's no such thing as writer's block. That was invented by people in California who couldn't write. **Terry Pratchett**

I often think of a poem as a door that opens into a room where I want to go.
  Minnie Bruce Pratt

Perhaps it would be better not to be a writer, but if you must, then write. If all feels hopeless, if that famous 'inspiration' will not come, write. If you are a genius, you'll make your own rules, but if not - and the odds are against it - go to your desk no matter what your mood, face the icy challenge of the paper - write.
J. B. Priestly

The makers of the short story have rarely been good novelists. V. S. Pritchett

Short stories can be rather stark and bare unless you put in the right details. Details make stories human, and the more human a story can be, the better.
  V. S. Pritchett

Whenever you feel an impulse to perpetrate a piece of exceptionally fine writing, obey it - and delete it before sending your manuscript to the press. **Sir Arthur Quiller-Couch**

Most beginning writers are like chefs trying to cook great dishes that they've never tasted themselves. How can you make a great bouillabaisse if you've never had any? If you don't really understand why people read mysteries, then there's no way in the world you're going to write one that anyone wants to publish. **Daniel Quinn**

When you send off a short story, it sits on the editor's desk in the same pile with stories by the most famous and honored names in present-day writing--and it's not going to be accepted unless it's as good as theirs. **Daniel Quinn**

Prune what is turgid, elevate what is commonplace, arrange what is disorderly, introduce rhythm where the language is harsh, modify where it is too absolute. **Marcus Fabius Quintilianus,**

Write quickly and you will never write well; write well, and you will soon write quickly. **Marcus Fabius Quintilianus**,

R

Words are a lens to focus one's mind. **Ayn Rand**

[Editors] drive us nuts. We go from near-worshipful groveling when we submit to bitter cursing when they reject us. **Ken Rand**

Writers are schizophrenic. On the one hand we tell ourselves, "This is a work of genius! I've created Art!" Then we try to peddle it, like a widget, to The New Yorker, Playboy, or SF Age. **Ken Rand**

I know that if I have been working on one paragraph and I have written it three times, it goes in the bin. Unless it comes straight out, it is wrong, it is awkward, it does not fit. **Robert Rankin**

Really, in the end, the only thing that can make you a writer is the person that you are, the intensity of your feeling, the honesty of your vision, the unsentimental acknowledgment of the endless interest of the life around and within you. Virtually nobody can help you deliberately -- many people will help you unintentionally. **Santha Rama Rau**

Writing is an occupation in which you have to keep proving your talent to those who have none. **Jules Renard**

Writing is the only profession where no one considers you ridiculous if you earn no money. **Jules Renard**

All of a writer that matters is in the book or books. It is idiotic to be curious about the person. **Jean Rhys**

Writers write about what obsesses them. You draw those cards. I lost my mother when I was 14. My daughter died at the age of 6. I lost my faith as a Catholic. When I'm writing, the darkness is always there. I go where the pain is. **Anne Rice**

Fundamentally, all writing is about the same thing; it's about dying, about the brief flicker of time we have here, and the frustration that it creates. **Mordecai Richler**

What is needed is, in the end, simply this: solitude, great inner solitude. Going into yourself and meeting no one for hours on end--that is what you must be able to attain. **Rainer Maria Rilke**

Every writer is a narcissist. This does not mean that he is vain; it only means that he is hopelessly self-absorbed. **Leo Rosten**

The only reason for being a professional writer is that you just can't help it. **Leo Rosten**

S

No fathers or mothers think their own children ugly; and this self-deceit is yet stronger with respect to the offspring of the mind. **Miguel de Cervantes Saavedra**

Poetry creates the myth, the prose writer draws its portrait. **Jean-Paul Sartre**

Engrave this in your brain: *EVERY WRITER GETS REJECTED*. You will be no different. **John Scalzi**

Don't mistake a good setup for a satisfying conclusion -- many beginning writers end their stories when the real story is just ready to begin. **Stanley Schmidt**

Resist the temptation to try to use dazzling style to conceal weakness of substance. **Stanley Schmidt**

If you don't know it, don't write it. **Darrell Schweitzer**

Writing isn't generally a lucrative source of income; only a few, exceptional writers reach the income levels associated with the best-sellers. Rather, most of us write because we can make a modest living, or even supplement our day jobs, doing something about which we feel passionately. Even at the worst of times, when nothing goes right, when the prose is clumsy and the ideas feel stale, at least we're doing something that we genuinely love. There's no other reason to work this hard, except that love. **Melissa Scott**

And as imagination bodies forth the forms of things unknown, the poet's pen turns them to shapes, and gives to airy nothings a local habitation and a name. **William Shakespeare**

Suit the action to the word, the word to the action. **William Shakespeare**

The road to ignorance is paved with good editors. **George Bernard Shaw**

delusive, and most transient of passions, they are required to swear that they will remain in that exalted, abnormal, and exhausting condition continuously until death do them part. **George Bernard Shaw**

The only way to avoid being miserable is not to have enough leisure to wonder whether you are happy or not. **George Bernard Shaw**

Some men see things as they are and ask why. Others dream things that never were and ask why not. **George Bernard Shaw**

A blank piece of paper is God's way of telling us how hard it to be God. **Sidney Sheldon**

Invention, it must be humbly admitted, does not consist in creating out of a void, but out of chaos; the materials must in the first place be afforded; it can give form to dark, shapeless substances, but cannot bring into being the substance itself. **Mary Shelley**

There are no rules in writing. There are useful principles. Throw them away when they're not useful. But always know what you're throwing away. **Will Shetterly**

Moving around is good for creativity: the next line of dialogue that you desperately need may well be waiting in the back of the refrigerator or half a mile along your favorite walk. **Will Shetterly**

Pay no attention to what the critics say; no statue has ever been erected to a critic. **Jean Sibelius**

Stories have a beginning, a middle and an end. But not necessarily in that order. **Robert Silverberg**

Writing is not a profession but a vocation of unhappiness. **Georges Simenon**

Reading and weeping opens the door to one's heart, but writing and weeping opens the window to one's soul. **M. K. Simmons**

Children read books, not reviews. They don't give a hoot about critics. **Isaac Bashevis Singer**

The wastepaper basket is the writer's best friend. **Isaac Bashevis Singer**

Editors also know that the people who are really readers want to read. They hunger to read. They will forgive a vast number of clumsinesses and scamped work of every sort if the author will delight them just enough to keep them able to continue. **William Sloane**

Writing for me is just like building a chair, making an artifact. The idea is that you build, create a story and cobble it together. If it stands up, that's good. If it stands up, it's comfortable, it's a good story, a good chair. **Scott Smith**

A great deal of talent is lost to the world for want of a little courage. **Sidney Smith**

The main question to a novel is - did it amuse? Were you surprised at dinner coming so soon? Did you mistake eleven for ten? Were you too late to dress? and did you sit up beyond the usual hour? If a novel produces these effects, it is good; if it does not - story, language, love, scandal itself cannot save it. It is only meant to please; and it must do that or it does nothing. **Sydney Smith**

The misuse of language induces evil in the soul. **Socrates**

We live under continual threat of two equally fearful, but seemingly opposed destinies: unremitting banality and inconceivable terror. It is fantasy, served out in large rations by the popular arts, which allows most people to cope with these twin specters. **Susan Sontag**

Why wouldn't you write to escape yourself as much as you might write to express yourself. It's far more interesting to write about others. **Susan Sontag**

By writing much, one learns to write well. **Robert Southey**

The first chapter sells the book; the last chapter sells the next book. Mickey Spillane

People are certainly impressed by the aura of creative power which a writer may wear, but can easily demolish it with a few well-chosen questions. Bob Shaw has observed that the deadliest questions usually come as a pair: "Have you published anything?" (loosely translated as: I've never heard of you) and "What name do you write under?" (loosely translatable as: I've definitely never heard of you). Brian Stableford

...the vital point to remember is that the swine who just sent your pearl of a story back with nothing but a coffee-stain and a printed rejection slip can be wrong. You cannot take it for granted that he is wrong, but you have an all-important margin of hope that might be enough to keep you going. Brian Stableford

Remarks are not literature. Gertrude Stein

Originality does not consist in saying what no one has ever said before, but in saying exactly what you think yourself. James F. Stephan

When two people are under the influence of the most violent, most insane, most What's hard, in hacking as in fiction, is not writing, it's deciding what to write.
Neal Stephenson

I write plays because dialogue is the most respectable way of contradicting myself. **Tom Stoppard**

If creative work protects a man against mental illness, it is small wonder that he pursues it with avidity; and even if the state of mind he is seeking to avoid is no more than a mild state of depression or apathy, this still constitutes a cogent reason for engaging in creative work even when it brings no obvious external benefit in its train. **Anthony Storr**

The only two kinds of books could earn an American writer a living are cookbooks and detective novels. **Rex Stout**

Like everyone else, I am going to die. But the words--the words live on for as long as there are readers to see them, audiences to hear them. It is immortality by proxy. It is not really a bad deal, all things considered. **J. Michael Straczynski**

When in doubt, blow something up. **J. Michael Straczynski**

Every writer must acknowledge and be able to handle the unalterable fact that he has, in effect, given himself a life sentence in solitary confinement. The ordinary world of work is closed to him -- and that if he's lucky! Peter Straub

A science fiction story is a story with a human problem, and a human solution, that would not have happened at all without its scientific content. Theodore Sturgeon

A short story...can be held in the mind all in one piece. It's less like a building than a fiendish device. Every bit of it must be cunningly made and crafted to fit together perfectly and without waste so it can perform its task with absolute precision. That purpose might be to move the reader to tears or wonder, to awaken the conscience, to console, to gladden, or to enlighten. But each short story has one chief purpose, and every sentence, phrase, and word is crafted to achieve that end. The ideal short story is like a knife--strongly made, well balanced, and with an absolute minimum of moving parts. **Michael Swanwick**

Whatever inspiration is, it's born from a continuous "I don't know." **Wislawa Szymborska**

T

In a novel, the author gives the leading character intelligence and distinction. Fate goes to less trouble: mediocrities play a part in great events simply from happening to be there. **Charles Maurice de Talleyrand-Perigord**

If you try to please audiences, uncritically accepting their tastes, it can only mean that you have no respect for them: that you simply want to collect their money. **Andrei Tarkovsky**

The only way to learn to write is to write. **Peggy Teeters**

No tale is so good...but can be spoilt in the telling. **Terence, 160 BC**

There are thousands of thoughts lying within a man that he does not know till he takes up the pen and writes. **William Makepeace Thackeray**

Not that the story need be long, but it will take a long while to make it short. **Henry David Thoreau**

How vain it is to sit down to write if you have not stood up to live. Henry David Thoreau

One writes such a story [The Lord of the Rings] not out of the leaves of trees still to be observed, nor by means of botany and soil-science; but it grows like a seed in the dark out of the leaf-mold of the mind: out of all that has been seen or thought or read, that has long ago been forgotten, descending into the deeps. No doubt there is much personal selection, as with a gardener: what one throws on one's personal compost-heap; and my mold is evidently made largely of linguistic matter. J. R. R. Tolkien

Drama, instead of telling us the whole of a man's life, must place him in such a situation, tie such a knot, that when it is untied, the whole man is visible. **Leo Tolstoy**

Fiction writing is great. You can make up almost anything. **Ivana Trump, upon finishing her first novel**

An essential element for good writing is a good ear: One must listen to the sound of one's own prose. **Barbara Tuchman**

Inside every fat book is a thin book trying to get out. **John William Tuohy**

I never started from ideas but always from character. **Ivan Turgenev**

As for the adjective, when in doubt leave it out. Mark Twain

Most writers regard the truth as their most valuable possession, and therefore are most economical in its use. Mark Twain

The test of any good fiction is that you should care something for the characters; the good to succeed, the bad to fail. The trouble with most fiction is that you want them all to land in hell, together, as quickly as possible. Mark Twain

Get you facts first, and then you can distort 'em as much as you please. Mark Twain

Substitute "damn" every time you're inclined to write "very;" your editor will delete it and the writing will be just as it should be. Mark Twain

The time to begin writing an article is when you have finished it to your satisfaction. By that time you begin to clearly and logically perceive what it is you really want to say. Mark Twain

A critic is a man who knows the way but can't drive the car. Kenneth Tynan

U

I learned that you should feel when writing, not like Lord Byron on a mountain top, but like a child stringing beads in kindergarten, --happy, absorbed and quietly putting one bead on after another. Brenda Ueland

My work…is to shatter the faith of men here, there, and everywhere, faith in affirmation, faith in negation, and faith in abstention from faith, and this for the sake of faith in faith itself. **Miguel de Unamuno**

The long-lived books of tomorrow are concealed somewhere amongst the so-far unpublished MSS of today. **Philip Unwin**

The measure of artistic merit is the length to which a writer is willing to go in following his own compulsions. **John Updike**

I want to write books that unlock the traffic jam in everybody's head. **John Updike**

V

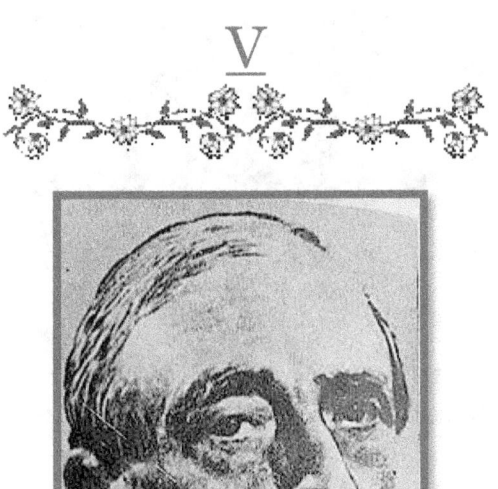

Follow the path of your aroused thought, and you will soon meet this infernal inscription: There is nothing so beautiful as that which does not exist. **Paul Valery**

You are what you read. **Esko Valtaoja**

I suspect that one of the reasons we create fiction is to make sex exciting. **Gore Vidal**

The adjective is the enemy of the noun. **Francois Marie Arouet de Voltaire**

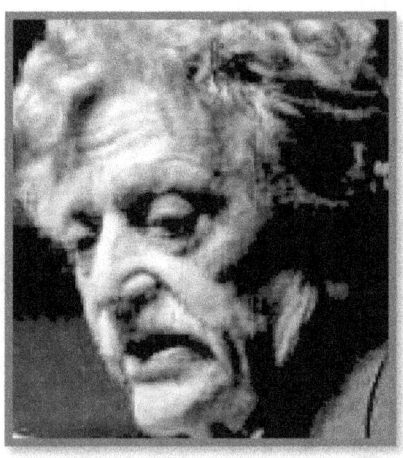

I guarantee you that no modern story scheme, even plotlessness, will give a reader genuine satisfaction, unless one of those old-fashioned plots is smuggled in somewhere. I don't praise plots as accurate representations of life, but as ways of keeping readers reading. When I used to teach creative writing, I would tell students to make their characters want something, even if it's only a glass of water. Characters paralyzed by the meaningless of modern life still have to drink water from time to time. One of my students wrote a story about a nun who got a piece of dental floss stuck between her lower left molars, and who couldn't get it out all day long. I thought that was wonderful. The story dealt with issues a lot more important than dental floss, but what kept readers going was anxiety about when the dental floss would finally be removed. Nobody could read that story without fishing around in his mouth with a finger. **Kurt Vonnegut, Jr.**

I have long felt that any reviewer who expresses rage and loathing for a novel is preposterous. He or she is like a person who has just put on full armor and attacked a hot fudge sundae or banana split. **Kurt Vonnegut, Jr.**

The art of writing is the art of applying the seat of the pants to the seat of the chair. **Mary Heaton Vorse**

W

The image that fiction presents is purged of the distractions, confusions and accidents of ordinary life. **Robert Penn Warren**

There is no idea so stupid or hackneyed that a sufficiently-talented writer can't get a good story out of it. **Lawrence Watt-Evans**

Imaginary evil is romantic and varied; real evil is gloomy, monotonous, barren, boring. Imaginary good is boring; real good is always new, marvelous, intoxicating. "Imaginative literature," therefore, is either boring or immoral or a mixture of both. **Simone Weil**

> The books we think we ought to read are poky, dull, and dry
> The books that we would like to read we are ashamed to buy
> The books that people talk about we never can recall
> And the books that people give us, oh, they're the worst of all.
> **Carolyn Wells**

A story isn't about a moment in time, a story is about the moment in time. **W. D. Wetherell**

No one can write decently who is distrustful of the reader's intelligence or whose attitude is patronizing. E. B. White

There is no satisfactory explanation of style, no infallible guide to good writing, no assurance that a person who thinks clearly will be able to write clearly, no key that unlocks the door, no inflexible rules by which the young writer may steer his course. He will often find himself steering by stars that are disturbingly in motion. E. B. White

A poet can survive everything but a misprint. Oscar Wilde

It is personalities not principles that move the age. Oscar Wilde

...I discovered that if I trusted my subconscious, or imagination, whatever you want to call it, and if I made the characters as real and honest as I could, then no matter how complex the pattern being woven, my subconscious would find ways to tie it together -- often doing things far more complicated and sophisticated than I could with brute conscious effort. I would have ideas for 'nodes', as I think of them -- story or character details that have lots of potential connections to other such nodes -- and even though I didn't quite understand, I would plunk them in. Two hundred pages later, everything would back-fit, and I'd say, "Ah, that's why I wrote that." Tad Williams

If the sex scene doesn't make you want to do it - whatever it is they're doing - it hasn't been written right. **Sloan Wilson**

I believe there are two ways of writing novels. One is mine, making a sort of musical comedy without music and ignoring real life altogether; the other is going right deep down into life and not caring a damn. **P. G. Wodehouse**

I never want to see anyone, and I never want to go anywhere or do anything. I just want to write. **P. G. Wodehouse**

(After being asked about his writing technique) I just sit at a typewriter and curse a bit. **P. G. Wodehouse**

You know what it means - you're a writer and you understand it. It's not just 'the satisfaction of being published.' Great God! It's the satisfaction of getting it out, or having that, so far as you're concerned, gone through with it! That good or ill, for better or for worse, it's over, done with, finished, out of your life forever and that, come what may, you can at least, as far as this thing is concerned, get the merciful damned easement of oblivion and forgetfulness. Tom Wolfe

Pay attention to the sound of words. Dave Wolverton

Characterization is an accident that flows out of action and dialogue. Jack Woodford

I count it a high honor to belong to a profession in which the good men write every paragraph, every sentence, every line, as lovingly as any Addison or Steele, and do so in full regard that by tomorrow it will have been burned, or used, if at all, to line a shelf. Alexander Woollcott

The more closely the author thinks of why he wrote, the more he comes to regard his imagination as a kind of self-generating cement which glued his facts together, and his emotions as a kind of dark and obscure designer of those facts. Reluctantly, he comes to the conclusion that to account for his book is to account for his life. **Richard Wright**

I'm writing a book. I've got the page numbers done. **Stephen Wright**

X

For me, writing [was] a question of survival...I could not trust anyone, even my family. The atmosphere was so poisoned. People even in your own family could turn you in. **Gao Xingjian** (Referring to the Cultural Revolution)

Neither Christ nor Buddha nor Socrates wrote a book, for to do so is to exchange life for a logical process. **William Butler Yeats**

It is my contention that a really great novel is made with a knife and not a pen. A novelist must have the intestinal fortitude to cut out even the most brilliant passage so long as it doesn't advance the story. **Frank Yerby**

Exercise the writing muscle every day, even if it is only a letter, notes, a title list, a character sketch, a journal entry. Writers are like dancers, like athletes. Without that exercise, the muscles seize up. **Jane Yolen**

A young musician plays scales in his room and only bores his family. A beginning writer, on the other hand, sometimes has the misfortune of getting into print. **Marguerite Yourcenar**

Z

Occasionally, there arises a writing situation where you see an alternative to what you are doing, a mad, wild gamble of a way for handling something, which may leave you looking stupid, ridiculous or brilliant -you just don't know which. You can play it safe there, too, and proceed along the route you'd mapped out for yourself. Or you can trust your personal demon who delivered that crazy idea in the first place. Trust your demon. **Roger Zelazny**

One of my standard -- and fairly true -- responses to the question as to how story ideas come to me is that story ideas only come to me for short stories. With longer fiction, it is a character (or characters) coming to visit, and I am then obliged to collaborate with him/her/it/them in creating the story. **Roger Zelazny**

Writing is thinking on paper. William Zinsser